Organza Hoop Art

Embroidery Techniques and Projects for Sheer Stitching

SARAH GODFREY

Landauer Publishing

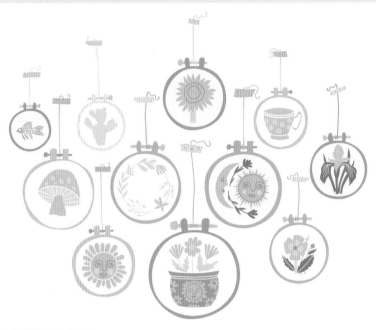

ORGANZA HOOP ART

Landauer Publishing, *www.landauerpub.com*, is an imprint of Fox Chapel Publishing Company, Inc.

Project Team
Editorial Director: Kerry Bogert
Editor: Amy Deputato
Copy Editor: Katie Ocasio
Designer: Llara Pazdan

Photographs by Sarah Godfrey and Pamarazzi Photography, Medina, OH. Some photos shot at Eastwood Furniture, Medina, OH. Additional photos: dablbabl/Shutterstock, 4, 95; Svetlana Kharchuk, 2, 6, 14, 36.

ISBN 978-1-947163-61-4

Library of Congress Control Number: 2020949192

We are always looking for talented authors. To submit an idea, please send a brief inquiry to acquisitions@foxchapelpublishing.com.

Printed in Singapore
24 23 22 21   2 4 6 8 10 9 7 5 3 1

Contents

Introduction 4

CHAPTER 1   Tools and Materials 6

CHAPTER 2   Stitch Glossary 14

CHAPTER 3   Projects 36

Ladybugs 38

Goldfish 42

Toadstools 46

Coffee Cup 50

Pink Poppies 54

Iris 60

Sunflower 64

Flowering Prickly Pear Cactus 70

Blue Flower Lady 74

Celestial Garden 78

Flower Lady Flowerpot 82

Floral Wreath 88

Thread Color Conversion Chart 94

About the Author 95

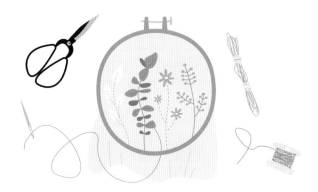

Introduction

This book will introduce you to the magic of hand embroidery on organza. Whether you are an established embroidery lover, or you have decided to start stitching for the first time, you will find techniques and projects in this book to get you excited about working with sheer fabric. Embroidery is a wonderful, meditative experience in which the use of different stitches creates an exciting interplay between color and texture on fabric. Working with organza takes this craft to a whole new level, calling for a heightened focus on neatness and adjustments to stitching techniques that result in eye-catching finished pieces. This book will guide you through all of the tools you need to get started, followed by techniques and projects designed for all skill levels to learn from and enjoy. One of the wonderful aspects of hand embroidery is that it is quite easy to get started and build your skills!

My mother-in-law, Irene, gave me the final spark of inspiration I needed to try hand embroidery, and she took me on my first trip to buy supplies. Soon after that, I remember showing her pictures of embroidery on organza, and I knew I had to try it—even as a beginner. The pieces you can create with this fabric are captivating, and I want to share its magic with you while making the techniques as accessible as possible. While it might seem intimidating to work on transparent fabric, the techniques you will learn in this book will demystify the process and help you develop exciting new approaches to embroidery art.

If you have stitched before, you will recognize the stitches used in the projects, but the way you use them will be taken to the next level. If you have never tried embroidery before, these projects will help you develop a precision that will only serve you in your next embroidery endeavors. While the fabric may be sheer, the weave is tough enough to handle the creative process—and even a few mistakes!

The book opens with an overview of the supplies you will need to get started and some key tips for success. Next, you will find an in-depth stitch glossary with illustrated instructions on the embroidery techniques you will use in the projects. The twelve vibrant embroidery projects are organized based on difficulty level, from easiest to most advanced. After reading this book and working through these pieces, you will not only have new approaches to the craft, but you will also have beautiful artwork to display in your home. Happy stitching!

Visit me on Instagram: *@thelakeofspring*

CHAPTER 1

Tools and Materials

Before you start stitching, you will need the right supplies. There are a few important considerations to keep in mind when choosing the best tools and materials for embroidering on organza, and this chapter will walk you through the items you will need and what to look for when choosing them. All of these supplies are readily available at craft and fabric stores, as well as online.

These are just a few of the many colors of organza fabric you can find.

Fabric

There are several different organza options available in fabric stores. When choosing organza for hand embroidery, there are a few key characteristics you want to look for: sturdiness, texture, and weave. Organza is an airy, transparent fabric with a beautiful, ethereal appearance. It is traditionally made with silk fibers and is used for various purposes, including clothing and home decor (such as drapes). Because it is a delicate, sheer fabric, you often see it overlaid onto heavier textiles.

Many of the organza options you will find in stores or online are synthetic blends, which are the most affordable. When you are selecting your fabric, take time to touch the different options and make sure you like the feel of the weave. I like my organza to feel silky and smooth but still sturdy. Some of the synthetic options I have tested

have a very plastic-like texture and fray very easily. If the texture is too slippery or too grainy, you may also run into issues with your writing tools when transferring a pattern. If the texture is not silky and has too much slip or roughness to it, I find that pencil markings crumble right off, and marker ink doesn't have an ideal surface to adhere to. It can be helpful to purchase a few small pieces to test different options and find the exact fabric that suits your preferences.

Organza also comes in a beautiful range of colors—anything from crisp white to pastel pink to rich jewel tones and even shimmery options. In this book, you will see me working with my favorite organza colors: white and soft blush pink. I have also used a few other colors, and I really like the results! It is a lot of fun to test out different colors for different projects.

SHEER FABRIC TIPS FOR SUCCESS

Working through a hand embroidery project on organza can feel a bit like working through a puzzle (in a good way!). As you will see, you may have to do a little bit of bending and weaving with your needle and thread to ensure your project is nearly as neat on the back as it is on the front. I truly love this part of working on organza. It is an exciting challenge that keeps your mind focused on the present while anticipating what the end result will hold. I promise you that the winding path you embark upon for each project will help you improve your stitch skills and create something very special. This added precision lends itself to a unique "wow" factor, making for pieces that spark curiosity and intrigue in fellow stitchers.

With all that in mind, to make the process as smooth as possible, I have a few tips for success when embroidering on organza:

Work over a bright, solid surface. Because organza is sheer, it can be challenging to see the markings on your fabric. To make the markings more visible, I suggest working over either a white or a bright solid-colored surface. My desk is white, which I find really helpful, but if I am sitting on the couch or on my bed, I put a pad of white paper under my work so I can see my lines more clearly.

Touch up your tracing as needed. Sometimes I find that I need to retouch my tracing so I can see my lines better when stitching. If the pencil lines fade slightly as I'm working on a project, I quickly retrace them so I don't have to strain my eyes to see my outlines.

Be careful with your hoop. When tightening your hoop and pulling the organza taut, you can push the weave of the fabric out of place, making it look uneven and threadbare in places. If this happens, as long as a hole hasn't formed, you can use the tip of your needle to gently scrape back and forth on the fabric and fix the weave. This also works well if you have had to unpick any stitches and are left with visible needle holes in your fabric. To protect your organza before stitching, you can wrap the inner circle of your hoop with twill tape so that the fabric glides more easily and doesn't get damaged when you adjust the tightness.

Avoid knots. Especially when I am working on delicate details, I avoid starting and stopping with knots when embroidering on organza. Instead, I start by leaving a thread tail and then stitching it down as I go to secure my work. When it is time to stop and rethread my needle, I simply weave through at the back of my work a few times and snip.

Practice makes perfect! My first organza piece was definitely not my best! I started working on sheer fabric as a beginner, and it came with challenges. I couldn't control my stitches very precisely, and my shapes didn't turn out quite the way I had drawn and imagined them. I pushed through and kept practicing, and very soon I was able to develop my technique and create work that I was very proud of (and still am today). It is OK to make mistakes! It is normal to unpick stitches, start sections over, or try a stitch a few times before you get it right. I am confident that, with practice, you will make something beautiful, and I hope this book will help you get there faster and with more ease.

Needles and Thread

For stitching on organza, I use needles and embroidery floss (thread) by DMC®. I use a fine needle because it makes smaller, less noticeable holes in my fabric. My favorite needle set is DMC's size 3–9 embroidery set because the different sizes offer great options for several types of fabric, including organza.

Embroidery floss comes packaged as individual skeins of each color, with thread made up of six strands (or 6-ply). I often use all six strands at once when I embroider because I love how it pops off the fabric and has a nice, fluffy look. When I want my work to be more detailed, or when I am working on a small design, I use only half of the strands—or sometimes even just a single strand—depending on the look I am trying to achieve. We will be practicing this process in the coming chapters.

DMC six-strand embroidery floss is readily available at craft stores and online. The brand offers an excellent selection of colors as well as other interesting options, like glitter thread, tapestry wool, and variegated floss.

> **Note:** For all of the projects in this book, I used DMC six-strand embroidery floss, and I've provided the color numbers for the thread used in each project. See the color conversion chart on page 94 if using Anchor thread or to substitute according to shade.

Hoops

To frame your pieces (both while working and after they are complete), you will need embroidery hoops. There are a range of different sizes and shapes on the market, but for the projects in this book, we will be using circles and ovals of various sizes. I personally prefer wooden hoops because of their natural look and their versatility. You can stain wooden hoops or even paint them in fun colors. We will be finishing all of the projects in this book in wooden hoops.

Sometimes people use hoops only while working and then choose to stretch the fabric and frame it a different way. When I work on clothing, I like to use plastic hoops because I find they are gentler on my garments when I pull my fabric taut. I don't like the look of plastic hoops

A selection of embroidery needles and floss on bobbins. Labeling the bobbins with your shade numbers will help organize your thread.

as much, but because I only use them while I work, their appearance isn't really important. In choosing your tools and materials, a lot of decisions come down to your preferences and what works best for you.

Marking Tools

To transfer your designs onto organza, you will need a reliable writing tool. As noted earlier, sometimes the texture of your organza can be problematic with certain marking tools. If the fabric you have chosen is too slippery or rough in texture, it can be difficult to get marker ink to adhere to the fabric's surface. When using a synthetic blend organza, I have also found that water-soluble marker ink can pool between the fibers and then transfer onto light-colored threads. In addition, some water-soluble fabric markers are too light in color to show up on this sheer fabric.

After much trial and error, my favorite marking tool is a regular old pencil. As long as the pencil isn't too hard or too soft, it marks the fabric very well and lasts throughout the project. It's important to note that pencil marks tend to be quite permanent. I've found that when I've tried to remove a mistake, even by washing it with soap and water, my pencil lines were still slightly visible.

Glue

To complete your project, you will need glue to back (add backing fabric to) your hoop. When I use opaque fabric for my embroidery work, I like to leave a border of fabric at the back and then gather the fabric with running stitch. I leave a tail when I start my running stitch, and again once I reach the end, and finish by tying the tails together into a bow. This way, I can untie the thread and remove my work from the hoop if I need to for any reason (for example, if I wanted to wash my finished project). This approach doesn't work with organza, however, because the excess fabric would show through to the front of your hoop and distract from your stitches.

Following are the two methods that I suggest, but you can also try different approaches and see what works best for you.

FABRIC GLUE AND CLIPS

For this method, you will need fabric glue, a paintbrush, and clips (clothespins work well). Use your paintbrush to paint a thin layer of strong fabric glue onto the back of the inner circle of your hoop. Apply the glue in small sections, press the fabric to the hoop with your fingers, and hold it tightly in place with craft clips. Once you've clipped all of the fabric into place, allow the glue to fully dry, then remove the clips so you can carefully trim the excess organza as close to the hoop as possible.

HOT GLUE

I like this method because it is fast and easy if you are careful. Remember that hot glue guns can get very hot, and it is easy to burn your fingertips as the glue seeps through the porous fabric. Work in small sections, apply a very thin line of hot glue, and carefully place the fabric on the glue. To avoid burning my fingers, I hold the edge of the fabric, pull it taut over the hoop, and lower it onto the glue. When you are done, use your scissors to trim right to the edge of the fabric.

Other Essential Tools

EMBROIDERY SCISSORS

A pair of good embroidery scissors, or snips, is an important tool. Embroidery scissors are small, with super-sharp blades that allow you to get nice and close to your fabric so you can neatly and precisely trim your floss. Embroidery snips are also handy when you need to unpick stitches that you would like to redo (for example, if you decide you don't like a color). Try snipping out a section of your stitches with regular scissors—it would be next to impossible not to cut a hole in your fabric! Embroidery scissors come in a wide range of whimsical colors and shapes, so I always enjoy adding new pairs to my collection.

EMBROIDERY STAND

A tool that can be very helpful if you spend long hours embroidering is a stand that holds the hoop for you while you work. Embroidery is such a wonderful, meditative craft that it is easy for the time to slip by once you're in a groove. Spending hours at a time looking down, holding your hoop steady, and performing repetitive motions with your hand can be hard on the body. A stand can help bring your hoop closer to eye level and give your non-dominant hand a break from constantly holding the hoop. Even with the stand, I recommend taking frequent breaks to stretch your hands and walking around the room to avoid overworking your muscles.

Embroidery scissors come in many fun shapes, and these are a few from my personal collection.

STORAGE CONTAINERS

As your collection of floss, fabric, hoops, and scissors grows, you will need somewhere to put everything! There are so many small pieces involved in embroidery, making it easy for your workspace to become cluttered and disorganized. I have several clear plastic tubs that I use to sort my supplies and then tuck away in my closet or on my desk. There are also containers you can use to organize your thread by color after winding it onto bobbins. I find that I don't have time to wind my floss, label the bobbins, and sort them this way—instead, I place my fresh skeins into my tubs. I also have a big vase full of scraps that I can pull from, and I often keep a bag or container of floss that is separated for a particular project. This is just one way to approach organization, but having some kind of system in place is definitely useful in keeping your supplies from getting lost or damaged.

LIGHTING

Hand embroidery is an art that requires a lot of concentration and fine detail work, so good lighting is essential to make your process as smooth and enjoyable as possible. I prefer working in bright natural light, but the nature of my schedule means that I create most of my art at night. I have made some unfortunate color choices that I didn't notice until the next morning because I was working in dim lighting—and I have learned my lesson. Now I tend to choose my floss in natural light, and then, if I stitch in the evening, I make sure to use a good lamp so I can properly see what I am doing. It is much better to work in suitable lighting than to strain your eyes and experience headaches while working on your craft.

CHAPTER 2

Stitch Glossary

The projects in this book will have you using a range of my favorite stitches. This chapter provides you with a glossary of all the stitches you will use in chapter 3, with detailed step-by-step photos. Knowing how to execute a range of stitches enables you to create varied textures, which is the magic of embroidery. Whether you want to create the appearance of fur on an animal, the details of the center of a flower, precise linework for lettering, or the veins of a leaf, there is a stitch to elevate the look of your design. By experimenting with stitches I find interesting, I'm able to add more depth to my work, and I have established a set of favorite stitches that I use in almost all of my stitch work. I am always open to learning if a technique catches my eye, and I hope this book inspires you to do the same.

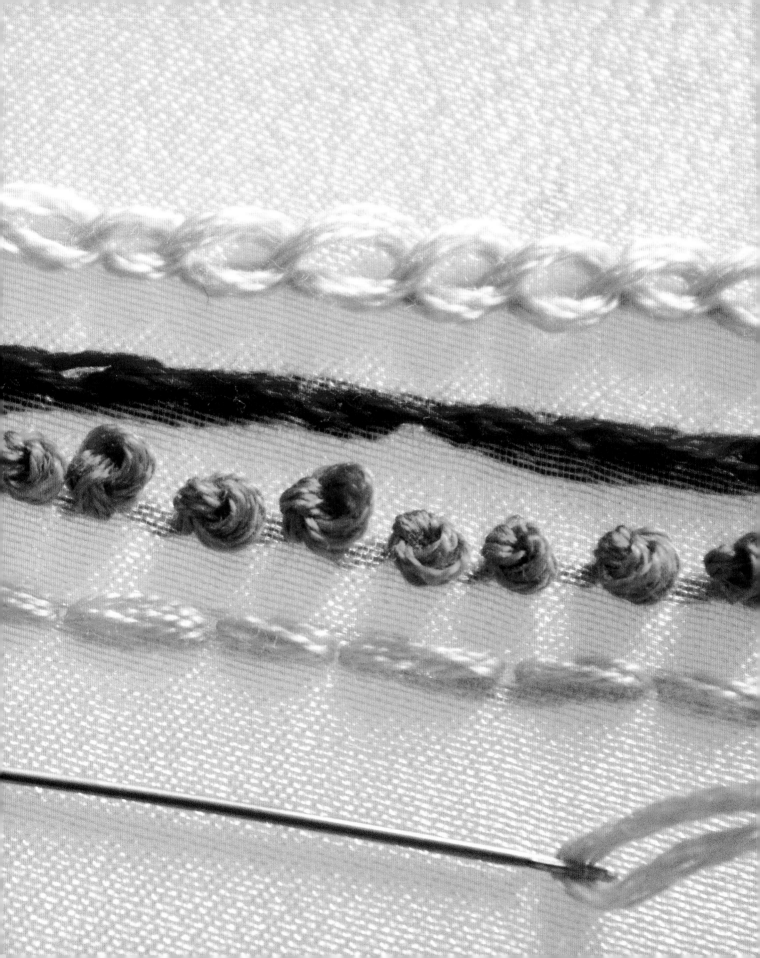

Back Stitch

Back stitch is one of the first stitches I would suggest learning. It is a simple stitch that produces thin lines that are perfect for outlining. My favorite use for back stitch is to outline satin-stitch shapes.

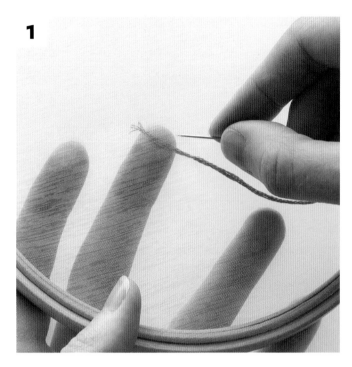

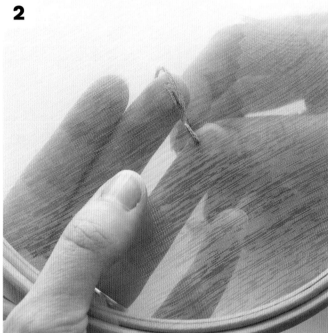

1. Come through your fabric from the back of the hoop. Next, push your needle back through your fabric a short distance away to make one small straight stitch. As you see here, I have left a small tail of thread that I'm holding in place at the back with my fingers. Make sure that you stitch this tail down so your work stays secure.

2. Come up with your needle again from the back of your hoop a short distance (one stitch length) away from the end of that first stitch. Make sure that the distance allows you to create a stitch of the same length as the first.

3

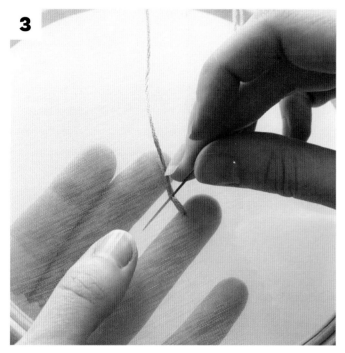

4

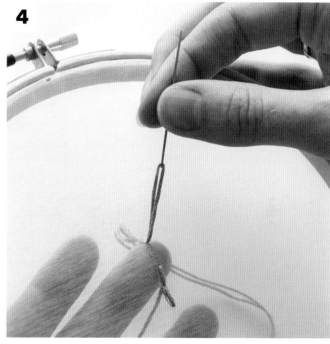

5

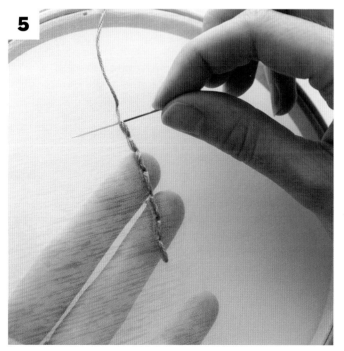

3. Put your needle back through the fabric right at the end of your first stitch, either using the hole that you already made there or making a new hole right beside that spot. Every time you make a new stitch, keep moving backward to where you ended with the previous stitch. This process of stitching backward makes your lines secure.

4. Once you master these first few steps, repeat them to form a line, either straight or curved.

5. As you work, focus on making the stitches as even in length as possible. When you are finished, weave your needle through the stitches you made at the back of your hoop to secure your work. By avoiding knots to start and stop, your embroidery will stay in place, and no loose threads will show through to the front.

Chain Stitch

Chain stitch creates a very interesting linked look, formed by creating lines of looped stitches. If you are looking to create lines with interesting texture for lettering, flower stems, or outlines, I highly suggest giving this stitch a try. This is a thicker line than what you would create with something like stem stitch, so I wouldn't recommend it for fine details.

Chain stitch is also great for filling areas. When you fill an area with chain stitch, you end up with rows of the stitch next to each other, and I really love the movement this creates. When you fill circles or other rounded shapes with chain stitch, you create a swirled effect, and I find that my eyes like to follow the rows inward.

1

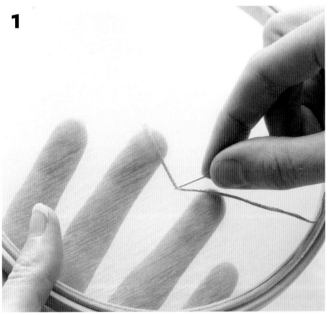

2

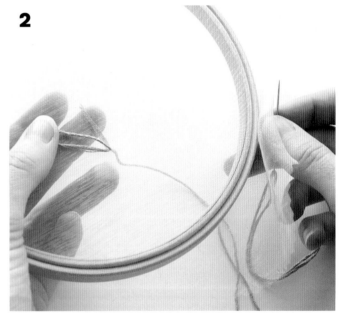

3

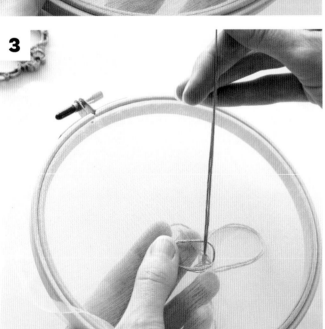

1. Come up through your organza from the back of your hoop. Put your needle back through the hole you came up through and start to pull the floss through to the back.

2. Continue to pull through until you are left with a small loop on the front of your fabric. Hold this loop steady with your thumb.

3. From the back of the hoop, bring your needle up through the fabric again at your desired stitch length away from your first hole. To do this, you will come up through the loop.

4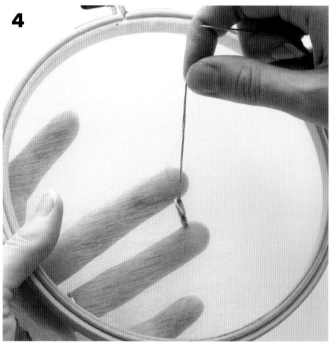

5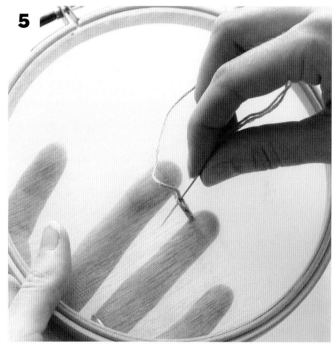

6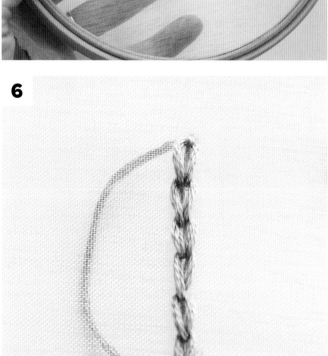

4. Make sure to pull through gently and stop when your loop lies flush with the fabric. Next, push your needle back into the fabric through the hole you last came up through.

5. Come back up through the fabric again to create a loop of the same size and pull gently to complete.

6. Continue these steps to form a line of loops that creates the appearance of a chain. When you are ready to end your line, anchor your last loop with one small straight stitch.

French Knots

Oh, French knots! They are not always the easiest to master, but once you nail the technique, creating them is addictive. This stitch has so many uses. Create it by wrapping your needle and then pulling it through the fabric, leaving a ball-like knot on the surface of your fabric. Decide how many times to wrap your needle based on how big you would like your knot to be. I tend to use all six strands when I embroider, but I drop down to three strands or fewer if I am working on a small area. I love this stitch for the center of flowers, but I have seen pieces done entirely in French knots (which requires a lot of patience!), and I love the rug-like effect it creates.

1. Start by coming up through your fabric with your needle and thread from the back of your hoop. If you are working on a large area and can hide loose threads, start with a knot, which is a little easier than beginning with a tail that you stitch over. Next, wrap your needle from one to three, or even four, times and gently pull on the floss to tighten it against the needle. Hold that tension with your floss and then place just the tip of your needle into your fabric.

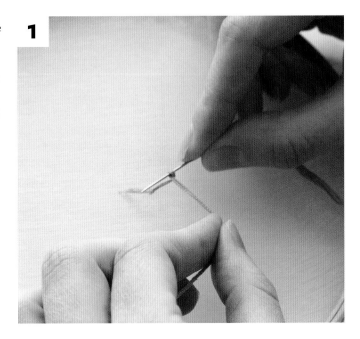

2. If necessary, pull your thread slightly tighter to the needle and slide the wrapped thread down to the surface of the fabric. Make sure your needle is inserted enough that the thread doesn't come loose.

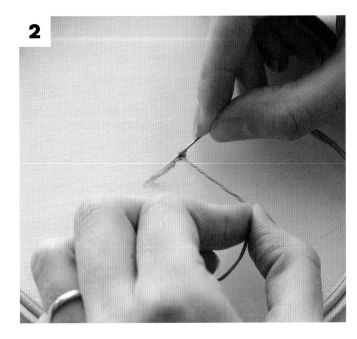

3

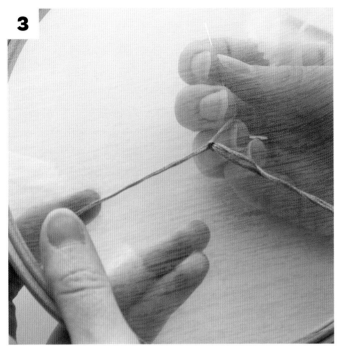

4

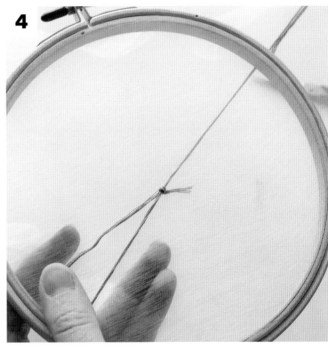

5

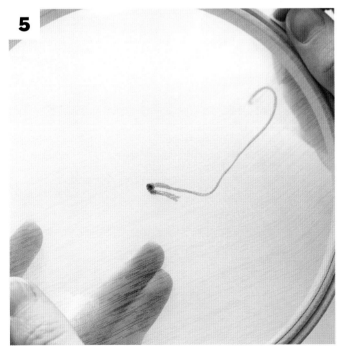

3. Start to pull your needle through to the back of your hoop. Be sure to hold your thread steady with your non-dominant hand. It is also important that you don't pull too tightly with this hand because the wrapped thread has to have enough space for your needle to pass through smoothly.

4. Keep your thumb on the loop of thread that forms to help gently guide it through. To form the knot, pull the trail of thread through the wrapped section you created with the needle.

5. Lift your thumb off the thread once the loop becomes very small and pull all the way through to complete the knot. Be careful not to pull too hard. Sometimes, when making a very small knot, you can pull it right through your fabric if you pull too hard.

Fringe Stitch (or Turkey Work)

The fringe stitch, also known as turkey work, is very similar to the pom-pom (see page 26), except you don't create a perfect ball. The first time I used fringe stitch was on a piece where I wanted an interesting way to create cactus flowers that jumped off the fabric. There are so many uses for this stitch: abstract pieces, floral embroidery, portraits, interior scenes (for example, to add fringe to a rug), animal art, and more. I simply create a row of loops held in place with locking stitches and then snip and trim them down to my desired length. If you want a subtle look, make fewer loops, and if you want a fuller look, stitch your loops densely and create multiple rows if needed.

1. Unlike most of the stitches discussed in this chapter, you will start by pulling your needle through your organza from the front to the back. Leave a tail, making sure it is the length you would like your fringe to be.

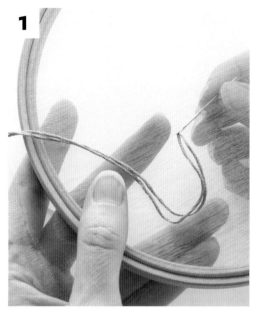
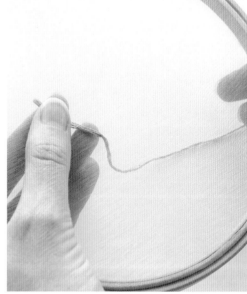

2. Pull your needle back up to the front, slightly past the tail you left, and make a small locking stitch to the left (over the tail).

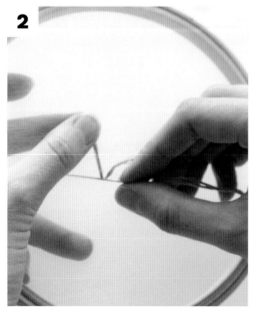
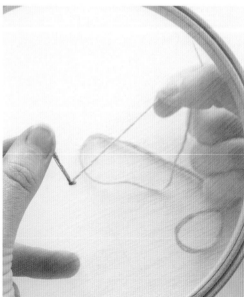

3

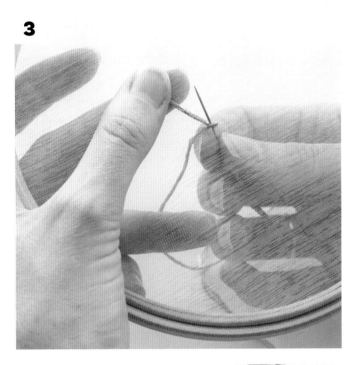

3. Come through again right beside the tail. You can see that my needle is coming up right at the top of my locking stitch, but I am careful not to make a gap at that spot.

4

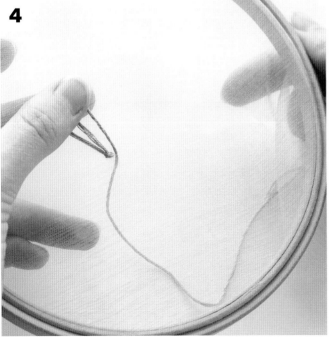

4. Pull your floss all the way through and then bring your needle down through the organza again, a short distance to the right of your locking stitch. Leave a loop that is the same length as your tail and hold it in place with your thumb.

6

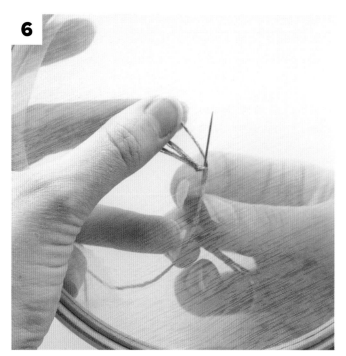

7

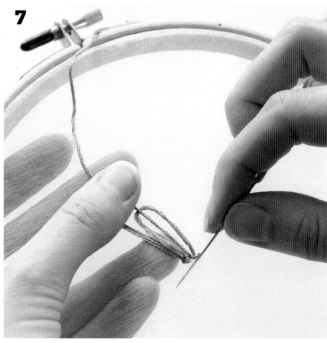

8

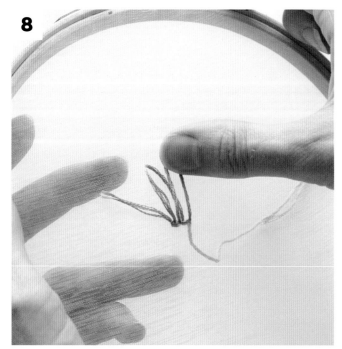

6. To keep the loop in place, make another small locking stitch over the end of the loop that you just pulled through.

7. Come back up again in the middle of your first loop and then pull your needle down through the fabric right beside your second locking stitch.

8. Do not pull all the way through but make a loop that is the same length as the first one you created.

9

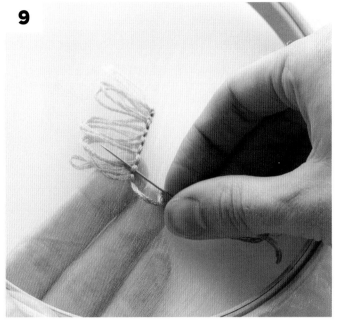

10

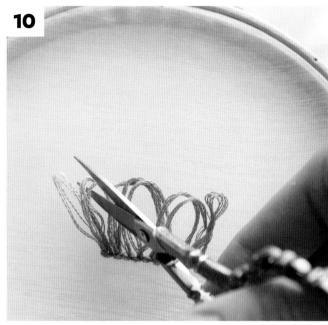

11

12

9. Repeat the process of making a loop and then locking it in place until you want to end your fringe. Flip the hoop over, weave your needle through a few times, and snip your excess floss.

10. Grab a pair of embroidery scissors and cut all the loops.

11. Use your needle to separate the six strands of floss and make the fringe look soft and fluffy.

12. Use your scissors to trim any areas you would like to even out.

Pom-Pom

If you want to add some height and fluffy texture to your work, learn how to create pom-poms. You can customize and create pom-poms big and small, and, I promise you, it is hard to resist reaching out and touching them once you're done! To make a perfect ball, fill in the center and any sparse areas with a series of loops. Then move on to the most fun part of this stitch: snipping the loops and giving the strands a haircut until you achieve a perfectly round appearance. This is a great technique for making interesting flowers, the fur of a cute animal, or part of an abstract piece. I hope you dream up something special for this stitch.

1. First, start by wrapping a long piece of floss around two or three fingers (depending on the desired size of your pom-pom). The more times you wrap, the fluffier and denser your pom-pom will be.

2. Leave a tail when you finish wrapping and then remove the floss carefully from your fingers. Wrap the tail around the coiled thread three times. You will end up with something that looks like a bow.

3

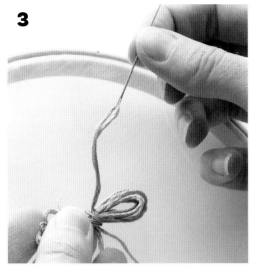

4

5

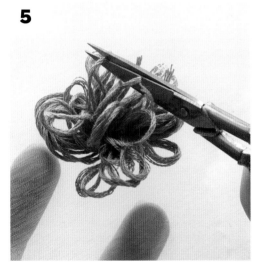

6

3. Thread your needle with a long (but manageable) length of floss. You can leave a knot at the end of this floss because the pom-pom will cover any stray thread. Take the bow you made, place it on the fabric at the desired location, and come up from the back with your needle in the middle of the bow. Use a couple of stitches to hold it in place.

4. Make a series of loops, focusing mainly on the center of the bow, to ensure that the pom-pom will have even density. You won't need any kind of locking stitch because the pom-pom becomes quite secure as you work and add loops. When are you are happy with the number of loops you have made, end by flipping over, weaving through a few times at the back of your work or making a knot, and then snipping the excess thread.

5. Trim your pom-pom into a fluffy ball. Start by cutting all of the loops. At first, the strands of thread might look shaggy and uneven.

6. Trim the cut loops until you are happy with the size and shape of your pom-pom. Use the tip of your needle to separate the six strands of floss so that your pom-pom looks extra fluffy.

Satin Stitch

Satin stitch might be my most-used stitch out of all the techniques I describe in this book. I love it because, when used effectively, it creates beautiful, smooth raised surfaces on top of your fabric, and it is great for filling in shapes. I also love how areas of satin stitch look next to each other, for example, when you mirror the angle of your stitches on each half of a leaf so that the stitches catch the light in a way that mimics natural veining.

Satin stitch can be tricky when you are first learning it. My biggest mistake when I first started was trying to fill large shapes with this technique, only to find that my stitches lost tension. The following step-by-step instructions include tips for making your satin stitch as smooth as possible.

1
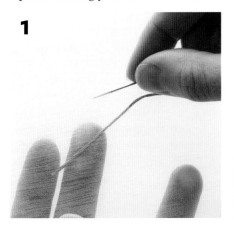

2
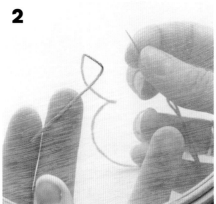

3
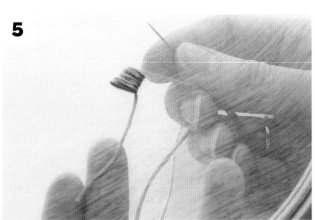

4

5

1. Pull your needle through from the back of the hoop to the front. Make sure to leave a tail of thread where you start.

2. Begin by making your first stitch. Think about the direction of your stitches and how that impacts of the look of your shape. You establish this direction with the first stitch you make. For example, when I make a leaf, my stitches angle upward on each half to create my desired texture.

3. Lay your next stitch smoothly beside your first and keep repeating to follow your shape. Stitch the tail down as you work on an individual shape or, if you know you will be working on another shape right against the area, you will stitch the tail down later. For this example, I used the latter approach.

4. When creating this shape, I did not draw an outline. When you do draw an outline, think about how you mark the fabric. If you use a marking tool that is not water soluble, you must bring your needle just beyond the outline to hide the markings.

5. It is also important to consider the tension and length of your stitches. Do not pull too tight or make very long stitches. If you pull stitches too tightly, it can cause the fabric to pucker, and if stitches are too long, they can warp.

Seed Stitch

To picture this stitch, imagine holding a handful of seeds and then scattering them onto the soil below. Seed stitch is made by randomly placing small straight stitches on your fabric. You can place them far apart or close together, depending on what you are aiming to achieve with your embroidery.

Ordinarily, if you were working on opaque fabric, you would have a lot of freedom to place your seed stitches either tightly together or far and wide. You could bounce around to different areas of your design with your stitches because the trail of thread wouldn't be visible on the front. Because this is not the case with organza, we will use seed stitch in a slightly different way for the projects in this book: we will place seed stitches of different colors close enough that they touch, allowing the colors to blend and form natural-looking texture (see page 67).

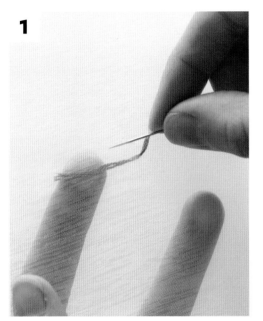

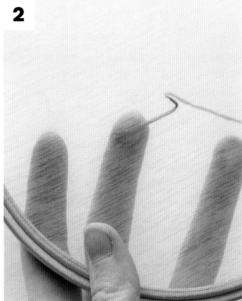

1. Come through from the back of the hoop to the front, leaving a small tail of floss at your starting point.

2. Push your needle back into the fabric a small stitch length away from where you came through.

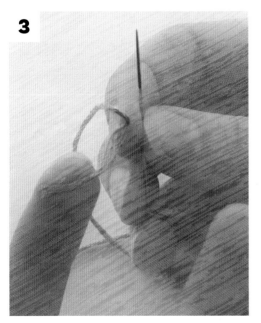

3. Pull your floss through to form one small straight stitch.

4. From here, continue to make small stitches, like seeds, scattered across your fabric organically.

Short and Long Stitch

Short and long stitch is the technique used in thread painting—possibly my favorite approach to hand embroidery. As the name suggests, this stitch involves making straight stitches, both long and short, to fill in shapes. To create that brushstroke effect and add dimension, blend colors from dark to light shades. Vary the length of stitches to add even more of an organic feel. This is a great stitch for filling large areas because you don't have to worry about the stitches warping as you do with satin stitch. You have a lot of freedom to choose the stitch length that will work best for you and achieve your desired effect.

1. Begin by pulling your needle through to the front of your hoop, leaving a small tail of thread that you will stitch down as you work. Make your first stitch at the desired length. (I started with a rather long stitch.)

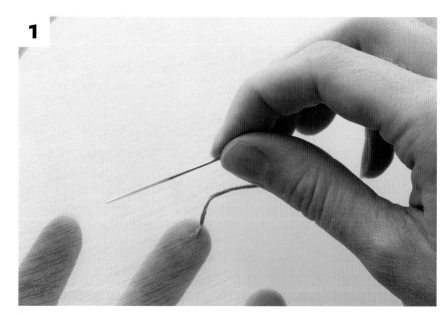

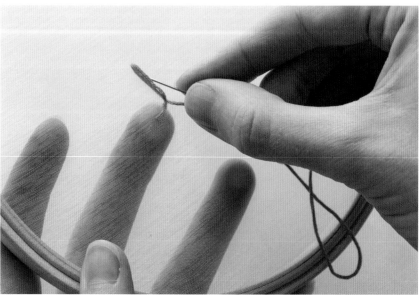

2

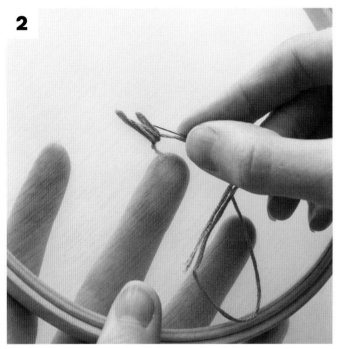

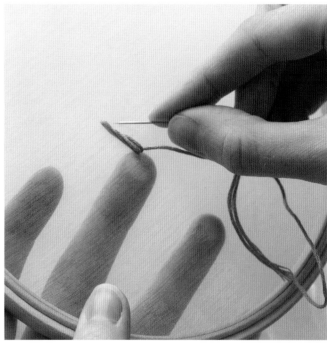

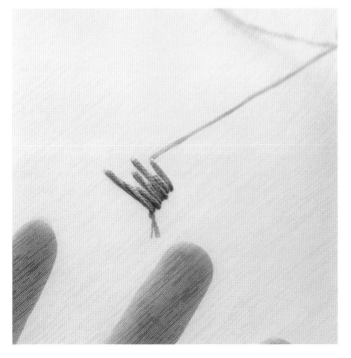

2. In keeping with the name, the next stitch is shorter. Your short stitches and long stitches don't have to be the same length each time. Repeat the process, alternating long and short stitches.

Thread Painting

I use short and long stitch to blend colors as I would when painting (hence the name "thread painting"). I start with a dark color and keep repeating the previous steps until I am ready to switch to a lighter shade.

For these photos, I used just one color, but the projects that follow in chapter 3 will show you how to blend colors with this stitch. Essentially, you would continue by taking the next lightest shade and making short and long stitches right against (and into at times) the area you just finished. Repeat this until your shape is finished and you are satisfied with the dimension you created with your thread.

Split Stitch

If you like chain stitch, I have a feeling you will also love split stitch! It creates a very similar look but is even faster to execute. Split stitch is another versatile stitch that you can use for linework, text, or even filling in an area. I find that split stitch is great for creating a thinner, more precise line than chain stitch, which tends to be thicker unless you use fewer strands of thread. The process of creating split stitch is very similar to that of back stitch, except that you bring your needle into the stitch you just made, splitting the thread in half.

1. Start by coming through the back of your fabric to the front and make one small straight stitch. As you can see, I leave a tail, and I either stitch into it or make sure that it is covered with my next stitches so that my work is secure. This is especially important for keeping your work neat when making delicate lines on organza.

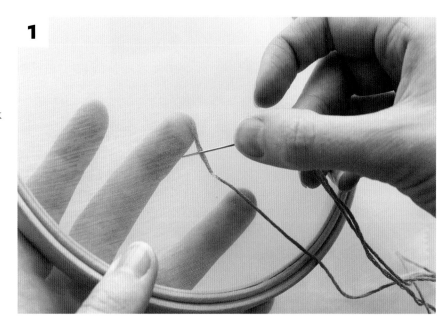

2. Next, come back up at your desired stitch length and instead of going down into the hole at the end of your first stitch, push your needle into the previous stitch, splitting the thread.

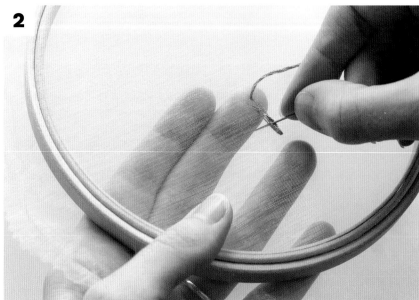

3

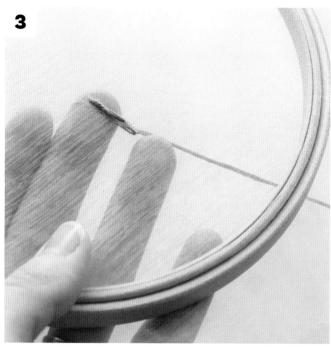

3. Pull through all the way and then keep repeating this process to form your line.

4. Make sure to keep your stitches the same size as you work, and you will end up with a thin embroidered line that looks similar to chain stitch. When you are done, weave your needle through the back of your line a few times to secure.

4

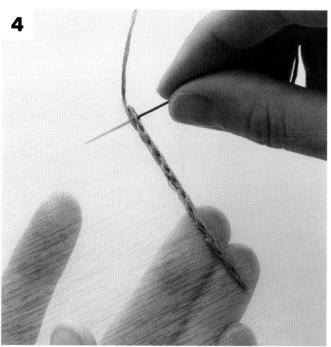

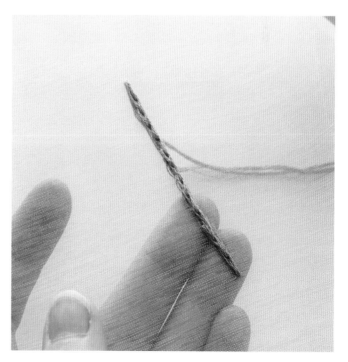

Stem Stitch

Stem stitch is a very popular and versatile stitch in hand embroidery. It creates a thin line that is perfect for nimbly navigating both curved and straight lines, so I included it here as an alternate stitch for creating flower stems, letters, outlines, and more. You can adjust the size of your stitches to suit the level of precision and intricacy required for your particular design. I recommend smaller stitches for tightly curved lines and detailed shapes.

1. Pull your needle and floss through to the front of the hoop and begin by pushing your needle back in, making a longer stitch than what you will use for the rest of your line. As usual, leave a tail that you can stitch down to secure.

2. Before pulling all the way through, leave a loop so that you can bring your needle back up through the fabric halfway between these two holes. Then pull your floss flush against the organza.

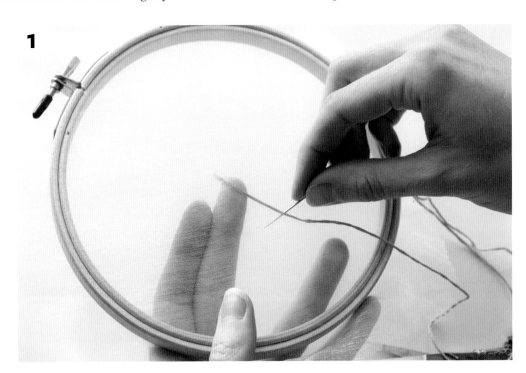

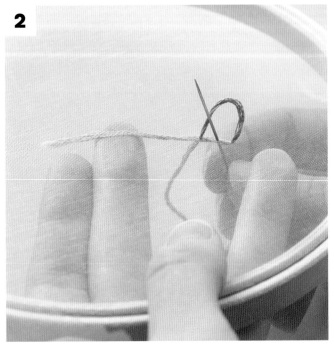

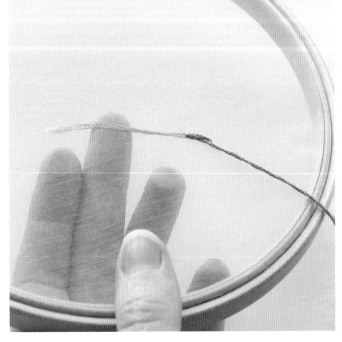

3

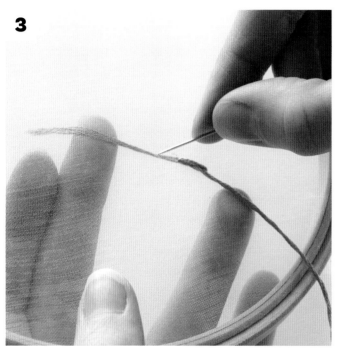

4

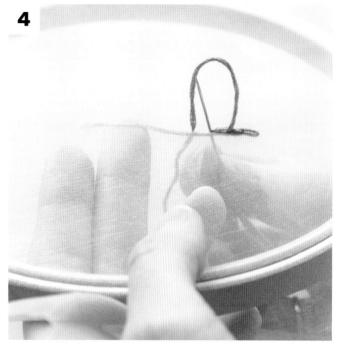

3. Push your needle back into the surface of the fabric, this time at your regular stitch length.

4. Bring your needle back up through the fabric, coming through right at the end of your previous stitch. Remember, the very first stitch was longer, so you came through halfway to make all of the stitches even. Come up through the loop exactly the same way each time—I came up to the left of the loop—to ensure that the line is smooth.

5

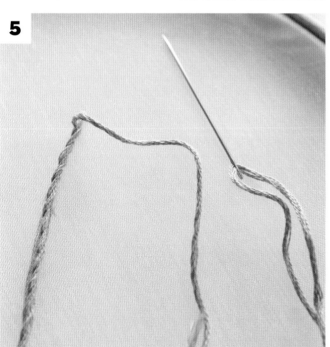

5. Keep repeating the process explained in steps 3 and 4 until your line is complete. At the back, weave your needle and thread through a few times before snipping off the excess floss.

CHAPTER 3

Projects

Now that you have learned about the materials and techniques required for stitching on organza, it is time to put that knowledge into practice! This chapter contains twelve exciting projects, with step-by-step instructions and accompanying photographs, using the stitches outlined in chapter 2. Each project also includes a pattern for easy tracing. The designs are organized based on difficulty, from easiest to more advanced. Work through them in order, or mix it up and try what piques your interest first—the practice will only help you build your skills!

Note: In chapter 1, I discuss backing your hoops. This is an essential step in my creative process with organza embroidery, and it is how I finished all of the projects in this book. Please see page 11 for instructions on this final step.

Ladybugs

This is a fun piece of hoop art that you can easily complete as a weekend project. Because it is a smaller project, you will be stitching in tighter areas and working on some fine detail. To keep the work neat and detailed, split your floss in half from 6-ply to 3-ply. Being attentive to detail is worth it for this little gem of a project. When you hold the finished piece up to the light, these critters create shadows that look as if they are crawling up your wall!

SUPPLIES
- Thread colors (DMC): 310, ECRU, 817
- Hoop: 4" (10.2cm)
- Fabric: 6" (15.2cm) square

STITCHES USED
- Satin stitch (see page 28)
- Short and long stitch (see page 30)
- Split stitch (see page 32)

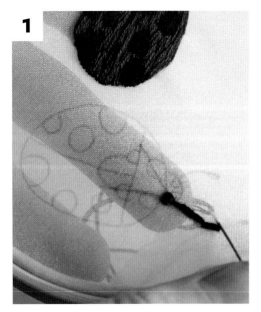

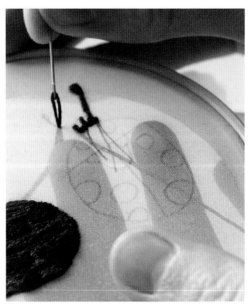

Note: The key area where you need to keep an eye out for stitches showing through to the front is the antennae. This is the trickiest part of this pattern, but once you finish it, you will have much more forgiving areas to work with!

1. Fill in half of the small head area (leaving space for the eyes) with satin stitch in 310, then make one antenna with a small straight stitch followed by two or three small split stitches. Complete the antenna with a small oval at the top made of three or four satin stitches. Make your way back down to the head by turning your hoop over and weaving through the stitches you just made. Then stitch the rest of the head and make the second antenna in the same way as the first.

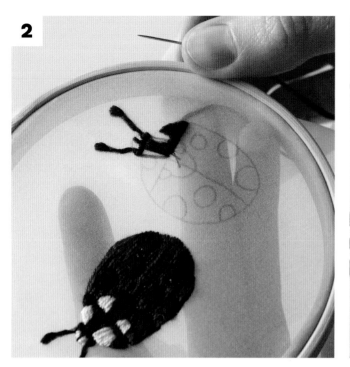

2

2. Use satin stitch to fill in the black area at the top of the ladybug's body, leaving space for the white spots. Next, stitch the large black spot in the center of the body, then the central line where the ladybug's wings come together with split stitch, and then the small black spots on the wings; when you stitch the red sections in the next step, they will hide the trail of thread. Finish by weaving through at the back a few times and snipping the thread.

3. Satin stitch the white spots with ECRU: start with the two on the wings, then the two on the body, and finally the two small spots on the head. Stitching in this order makes it easier to secure the tail and ensures that you have an area to secure your thread when you are done.

3

4

4. Add the bright red that makes this design pop! Use short and long stitch in 817 to fill in the wings and create a smooth appearance. Be sure to blend your stitches into each other and densely fill the red areas.

― LADYBUG PATTERN ―

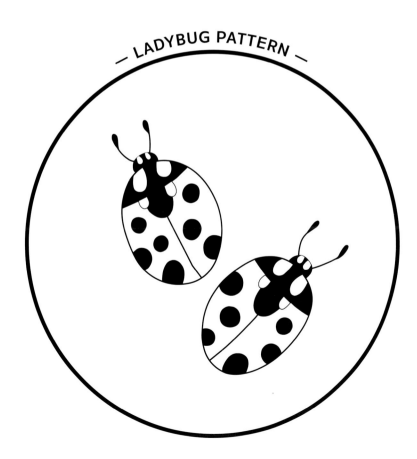

Goldfish

I have always thought that fish make the perfect subject matter for organza. The fabric is clear, like water, and that transparency gives shapes a sense of buoyancy. This cute goldfish looks like it is ready to swim away, and I love the oval hoop that perfectly suits the shape of the fish's body. With cheery shades of orange, this piece would be adorable for a child's room—or for anyone who loves aquatic life! As this is a smaller project, you will be using three strands of floss throughout the process.

SUPPLIES	STITCHES USED
• Thread colors (DMC): 742, 970, 3853, 921, ECRU, 310, 3856 • Hoop: 3½" x 6" (8.9 x 15.2cm) • Fabric: 8" (20.3cm) square	• Satin stitch (see page 28) • Split stitch (see page 32)

1

Note: It can be tricky to keep track of the lines you traced for the individual scales (unless you stop and start with each scale). Retrace your pencil markings as needed, or take one or two strands of thread and use back stitch or split stitch to outline the scales before starting your satin stitch.

1. Stitch the scales using satin stitch in 742, 970, 3853, and 921. Randomly select the colors as you stitch, creating an even mix throughout the design.

2. Stitch the head of the fish in satin stitch, using 742. Keep your work as smooth as possible as you maneuver around the space for the eye.

3. Use ECRU to satin stitch a circle for the white of the eye. Use 310 to make the pupil in the center with a few small stitches. Outline the eye with split stitch in ECRU.

4

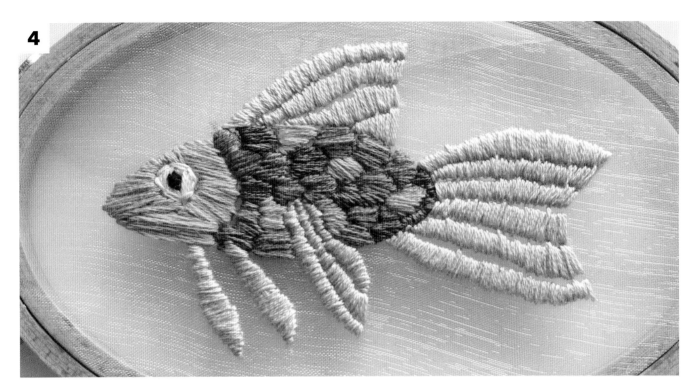

4. To create the fins, use satin stitch in shade 3856. The striped effect helps catch the light and mimics the natural texture of a fish's fins.

– GOLDFISH PATTERN –

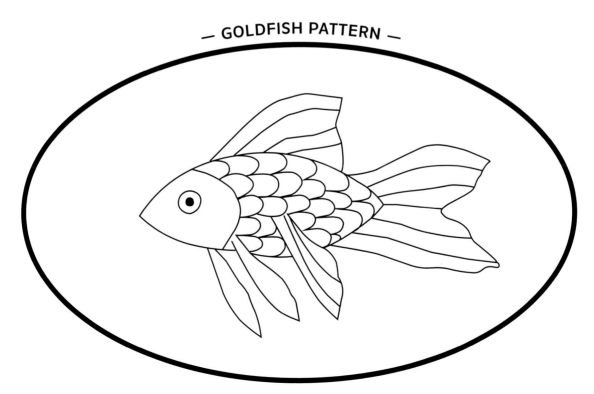

Toadstools

There is nothing more magical to me than going for a nature walk and spotting wild mushrooms along the forest floor. I grew up loving fairy tales and folklore (and still do), and mushrooms never fail to captivate my imagination. This design uses an oval hoop, which perfectly complements the tall, sculptural form of the toadstools. This project allows you to tap into your sense of whimsy while creating something that brings nature into your home.

SUPPLIES	STITCHES USED
• Thread colors (DMC): 321, 815, ECRU, 3864, 613, 3031 • Hoop: 7¾" x 4¾" (19.7 x 12.1cm) • Fabric: 9¾" (24.8cm) square	• Back stitch (see page 16) • Satin stitch (see page 28) • Short and long stitch (see page 30)

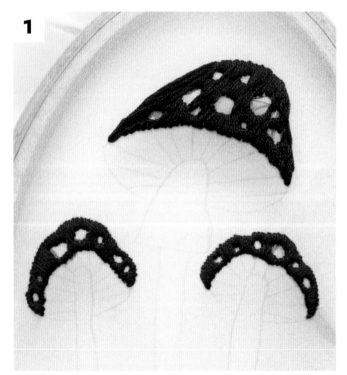

1. Use satin stitch in 321 to fill in the top sections of the two smaller toadstools, leaving space for the spots. Create some dimension by shading the top section of the largest mushroom. Starting at the bottom edge of the mushroom top, use short and long stitch in 815 to stitch about halfway up. Next, blend into the deep red with 321, again using short and long stitch, and work up to the top of the mushroom.

2. Fill in the white dots with satin stitch in ECRU.

3

3. Begin shading the gills using shade 3864 to create diagonal short and long stitches that radiate out from the stem of each mushroom. Although you will stitch over your traced lines, they act as a helpful guide. Then switch to shade 613, blending with short and long stitch again until you reach the bottom of the red sections you just finished.

4

5

4. Stitch the rounded triangular shape at the top of the large mushroom's stem, below the gills. Start with short and long stitches in 3864 that frame the top, bottom, and outer edge of the shape. Blend 613 into these stitches and then use ECRU to highlight the middle.

5. Stitch the stems with horizontal satin stitch. Use 613 for the center mushroom and ECRU for the smaller mushrooms.

6

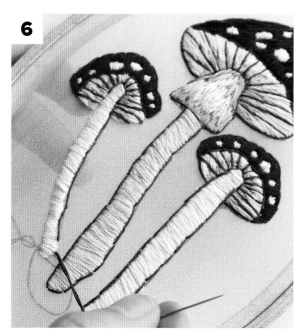

6. Split 3031 into three strands (3-ply) and use back stitch to outline each mushroom. Add diagonal lines to the gills to create more detail and contrast.

— TOADSTOOLS PATTERN —

Coffee Cup

If you are anything like me, you enjoy a cup of coffee or tea to start your day. And I know I am not alone in enjoying a good cup of coffee while I embroider. What makes the experience that much more special is having a beautiful cup to sip from. This is a perfect weekend project, small enough to pop into your bag and take with you on the go. The use of split stitch for the coffee and the polka dots creates an interesting look that draws the eye to these design features. When finished, this hoop would look great hanging in an office or leaning on a bookshelf in a reading nook.

SUPPLIES	STITCHES USED
• Thread colors (DMC): 333, 155, 3862, 211, ECRU • Hoop: 4" (10.2cm) • Fabric: 6" (15.2cm)	• Satin stitch (see page 28) • Split stitch (see page 32)

1. Make vertical satin stitches for the purple borders: use the darker purple, 333, for the top of the rim, and the medium purple, 155, for the bottom of the rim and the bottom of the cup.

1

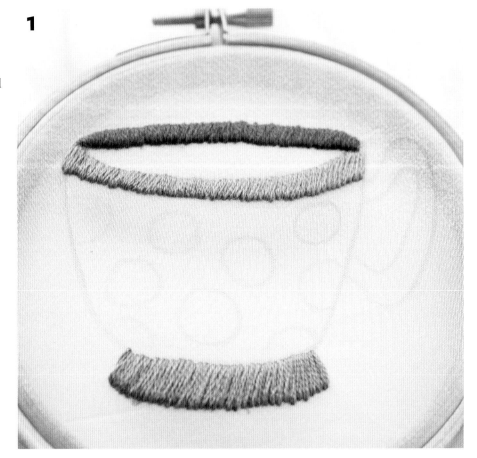

2. Use split stitch for the coffee in 3862 and for the polka dots in 211 to create a variation in texture. For each of these shapes, start along the outer edge and work your way inward to create a tight swirl.

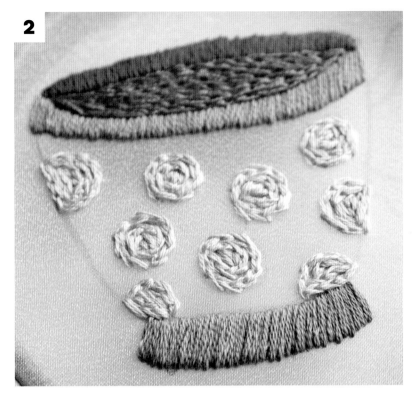

3. Stitch the cup and handle using satin stitch in ECRU. Keep your stitches as smooth as possible while maneuvering between the polka dots.

– COFFEE CUP PATTERN –

Pink Poppies

With bright pops of pink and hints of delicate detail, this pink poppy design is vibrant and lively. You will use satin stitch to create smooth surfaces and some simple thread painting to add shading. The details in the center of the flower and the shading of the petals are what make this design come alive. You will mostly be using all six strands of your thread (6-ply), but a few of the special details require 3-ply thread for precision. This bright and happy piece will add a touch of spring to your home decor.

SUPPLIES
- Thread colors (DMC): 310, 603, 225, 3863, ECRU, 895, 163, 368
- Hoop: 6" (15.2cm)
- Fabric: 8" (20.3cm) square

STITCHES USED
- Satin stitch (see page 28)
- Short and long stitch (see page 30)

1. Start with the main flower, using short and long stitch in 310 to create a smooth, dark surface on the inner areas of the petals. I start from the center of the flower and work my way outward, toward the end of each black section.

2. Use short and long stitch for simple thread painting on the pink petals. Begin with shade 603 and create stitches of varying length radiating out from the center of each petal. Next, blend with the lighter shade 225. Work the lighter pink into the darker pink stitches, moving outward to the edge of each petal and creating clean edges.

Note: As you reach the outer edges of the petals with the lighter pink, it may feel a bit like satin stitch because the stitches won't be as random as they were with the darker pink. Also, with the lighter pink, you may need to do a little weaving at the back to make sure that your thread doesn't show through as you move between petals.

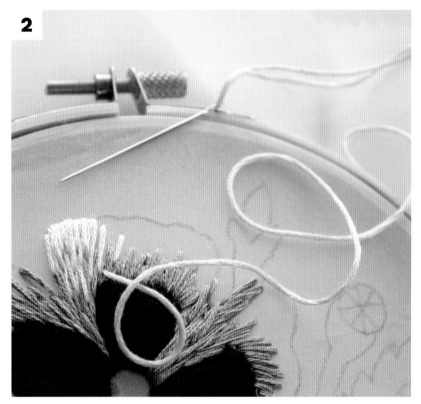

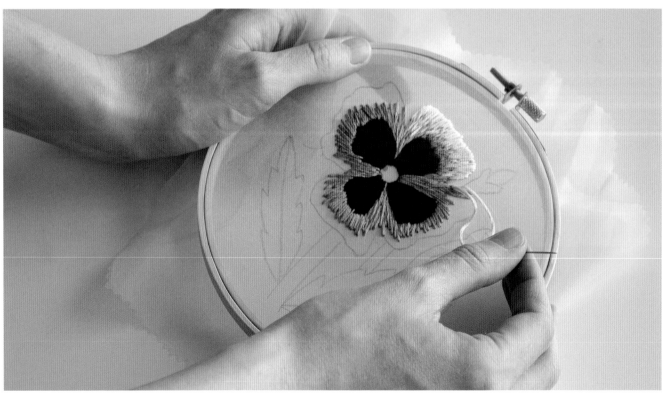

3

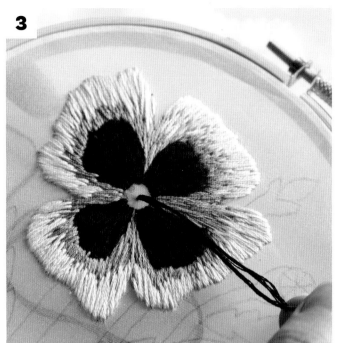

3. With black thread (310), come through the middle of the small circle in the center of the poppy and make a cross. Use two stitches, side by side, for each of the four small lines. Then, with 3863, fill in the rest of the circle with two to four small stitches in each of the four spaces. This approach, rather than a solid circle, more accurately represents the center of a real poppy.

4

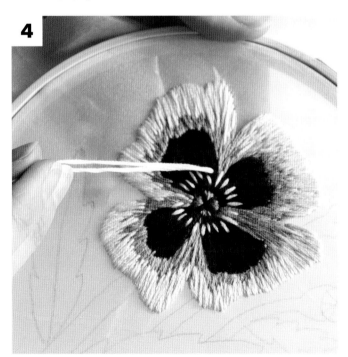

4. Use ECRU to add a ring of short stitches, spaced slightly apart, around the center circle to mimic the anthers of a poppy.

5

5. Use simple horizontal satin stitches in 895 all along the long, straight line of the stem.

6

6. Next, move on to the large leaves, using a similar method to the thread painting you did with the petals in step 2. Start along the central line of the leaves, making diagonal short and long stitches in shade 163. Switch to 368 for the outer edges of the leaves, creating a smooth shape with blended shading.

7

8

7. As you did with the stem of the large poppy, use horizontal satin stitch in 895 to fill in the other two stems.

8. For the bud on the center stem, start with short and long stitches in 603, then blend short and long stitches in 225 to give the bud a look similar to that of the petals. For the top of the righthand stem, start with 163 to create the darker green lines radiating out from the center, using two stitches for each of the eight short lines, and then fill in the circle with 368 (similar to how you made the center of the poppy). Finally, create the small leaf on the righthand stem using satin stitch. Simply follow the central line of the leaf, creating an angle on each side of the line and following it as you fill in the shape.

— PINK POPPIES PATTERN —

Iris

This delicate yet striking design will feel like you're working on a painting as you blend one color into the next with short and long stitch. The contrast between the pops of yellow and white against deep, cool-toned purples is truly eye catching. Each step acts like the stroke of a paintbrush, filling in the unique structure of the iris's petals. It is fun to play with these refined shapes and add details to the flower.

SUPPLIES

- Thread colors (DMC): 904, 581, 472, 25, 211, 340, 725, ECRU, 333, 154
- Hoop: 6" (15.2cm)
- Fabric: 8" (20.3cm) square

STITCHES USED

- Back stitch (see page 16)
- Short and long stitch (see page 30)
- Split stitch (see page 32)

1

2

3

1. Begin with the three long leaves that surround the flower. Start with the darkest shade, 904, focusing on the bottom and top of each leaf with short and long stitch. Next, blend in 581, again toward the top and bottom of each leaf, and finish with 472 in the center. This creates the shading we want in this part of the design.

2. Move to the stem. Use 904 to make short and long stitches, bringing the color up to the point where the two large petals split off from the stem. Next, blend in 581 and then finish with 472 at the top of each side of the stem. Notice how the short and long stitches do not end in smooth lines; instead, they end in a way that allows the next color to blend in.

3. Use short and long stitch for the small purple petal at the top of the stem, where the large petals split off. Start with the lightest purple, 25, followed by 211, and finishing with the medium purple, 340.

4. On each side of the small central petal you just made, blend 725 into the light green at the top of the stem. Bring the yellow up to the arch of each petal and then down slightly.

5. Blend ECRU into the yellow and then transition to 211, followed by 340, and then 333 as you work your way to the end of each petal.

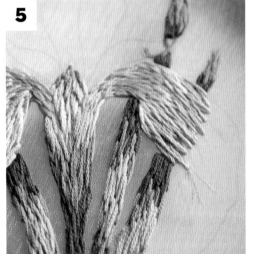

6. Stitch the two small purple petals, working from dark to light: 333, then 340, and then 211 out to the tips. Start the large central petal with a pop of 725 at the base of the small purple petals.

7

8

7. Blend 211 into the yellow, followed by 340 and then the darker 333 up toward the top of the petal to finish the shape.

8. Split a long strand of 154 in half so you are working with 3-ply floss, and use it to add dark veining to the base of the three large petals with split stitch or back stitch (or alternating between them as needed). Build detail until you are happy with the effect.

— IRIS PATTERN —

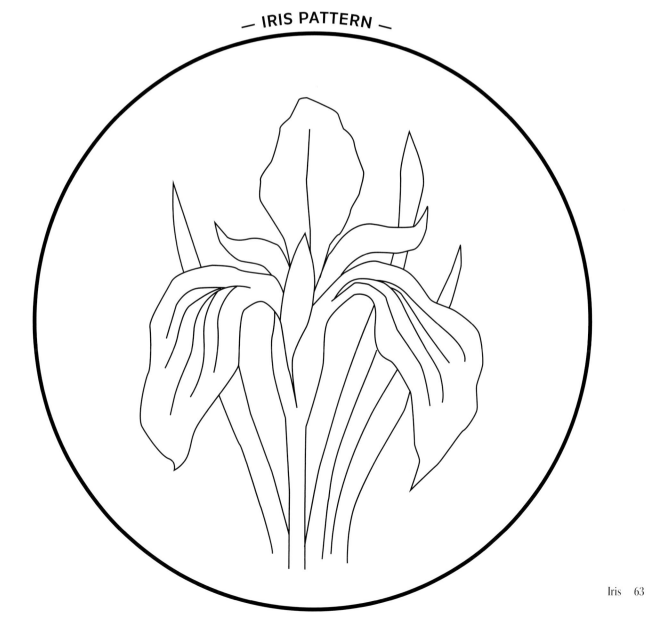

Sunflower

This bright and sunny 6" (15.2cm) project adds a beautiful pop of color to your space and creates a visually interesting mix of textures. Satin stitch, thread painting, and French knots give this piece a lifelike appearance with vivid bursts of yellow. Once you see the raised French knots and the smooth surfaces of your stitches, it will be hard not to reach out and touch this one! This design brings the warmth and magic of the cheerful sunflower into your home.

SUPPLIES	STITCHES USED
• Thread colors (DMC): 3347, 734, 831, 300, 310, 3852, 3821, 973 • Hoop: 6" (15.2cm) • Fabric: 8" (20.3cm) square	• French knots (see page 20) • Satin stitch (see page 28) • Seed stitch (see page 29) • Short and long stitch (see page 30)

1. Start with the stem, using shade 3347 to make horizontal satin stitches up to the beginning of the petals. You can see where the thread crosses the space between the top areas of the stem, but this trail will not be visible after you fill in the petals. Finish by weaving through a few times on the back side of your stitches and snipping off the extra thread.

1

2

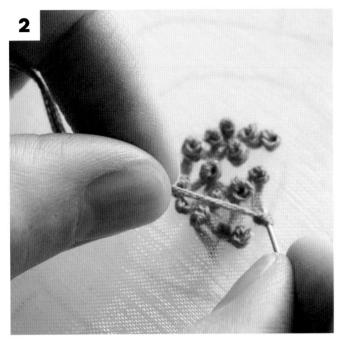

2. Begin with the smallest center circle. Use a knot to start your stitches—it will become hidden as you work, and a knot is much easier to work with than a tail when making the first French knots. Start with 3347 and randomly create French knots of various sizes, switching up how many times (one to three) you wrap your needle. When you are happy with how many knots you've made with 3347, fill in the remaining spaces with 734.

Note: I like to stitch the center before the petals because I find that it helps anchor the thread-painting process of creating the petals. The mix of French knots and seed stitches makes the center of the sunflower feel realistic and helps me visualize how the project will come together as I am stitching the petals.

3

3. Move out to the ring around the small inner circle. This is a very similar process to step 2, except you will use only one color, 831. Fill in this whole area with French knots, varying the number of times you wrap the needle, from one to three times.

4

4. Make seed stitches of various lengths to create texture around the ring you just stitched, beginning with 300 and then filling in the remaining spaces with 831.

5

5. Add extra dimension by outlining the ring of French knots with French knots in 310. Wrap your needle once or twice and place the knots a bit randomly for an organic feel.

6. Working on the petals from dark to light, begin right against the outer ring of the center of the flower with 3852, and make short and long stitches all the way around. Next, blend with 3821 and finish the end of each petal with 973.

7. Optional: Give the petals an even cleaner edge by outlining them with two or three strands of 973, using back stitch or split stitch. (This example is not outlined.)

— SUNFLOWER PATTERN —

Flowering Prickly Pear Cactus

Cacti understandably captivate the hearts of plant lovers everywhere—they are striking and sculptural and require little water, making them easy-to-care for houseplants. This cactus is even easier! Inspired by flowering prickly pear cacti, this project involves thread painting, French-knot details, and bright yellow fringe to mimic the blooms. Make this for yourself or a plant enthusiast in your life.

SUPPLIES	STITCHES USED
• Thread colors (DMC): 3362, 580, 472, BLANC, 444	• French knots (see page 20)
• Hoop: 6" (15.2cm)	• Fringe stitch (or turkey work) (see page 22)
• Fabric: 8" (20.3cm) square	• Satin stitch (see page 28)
	• Short and long stitch (see page 30)

1. Fill the large segments of the cactus with short and long stitch to create dimension with three shades of green. Working from dark to light, begin with 3362 around the top and bottom of each shape. Next, blend 580 into the areas of 3362, and then use 472 in the middle. Use satin stitch in 3362 to create the very small green areas that act as the bases for the flowers.

2

2. Add white dots by making French knots with BLANC. Split your thread into 2-ply or 3-ply and wrap the needle twice to keep the knots small. Add as many or as few knots as you like until you feel that the composition looks balanced.

3

4

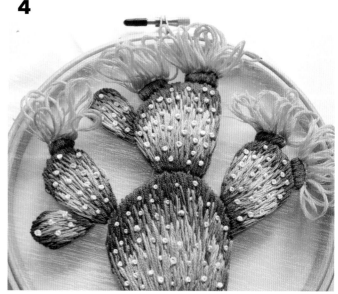

3. Using fringe stitch (turkey work), create the fluffy yellow flowers in 444. Atop each small satin-stitch area, create a series of loops held in place with locking stitches. Try to keep the loops a consistent length, slightly longer than you want the fringe so that you have room for error when trimming.

4. When you've finished making the loops, use your embroidery scissors to cut the loops open. Then use your needle to separate and fluff the strands of thread so they look less piecey.

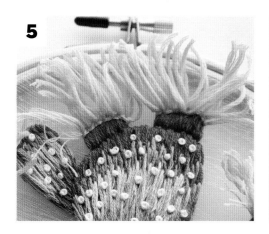

5

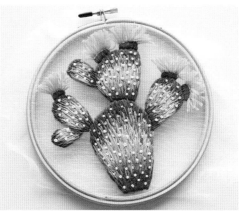

5. Trim the fringe until you are happy with the length. You can then use a piece of tape to gently lift off any tiny pieces of trimmed thread that are clinging to the project.

— FLOWERING PRICKLY PEAR PATTERN —

Blue Flower Lady

My flower lady designs remind me of what I was interested in drawing when I was a little girl, and my three-year-old son loves them! These designs are fun to make on organza; I love how their shadows look when light shines through to the wall behind. Enjoy creating this signature design of mine—I hope it makes you as happy as it makes me.

SUPPLIES
- Thread colors (DMC): 813, 827, 3753, 3766, 924, 3779, 760
- Hoop: 7" (17.8cm)
- Fabric: 9" (22.9cm) square

STITCHES USED
- Satin stitch (see page 28)
- Split stitch (see page 32)

1. Stitch each petal using horizontal satin stitches. Start the ring of petals above the outer edge of the left eyebrow. This is the color pattern that I used: three petals in 813, two petals in 827, three petals in 3753, two petals in 827, three petals in 3766, two petals in 813, three petals in 3753, two petals in 827, and finally three petals in 3766. This will bring you back to where you started.

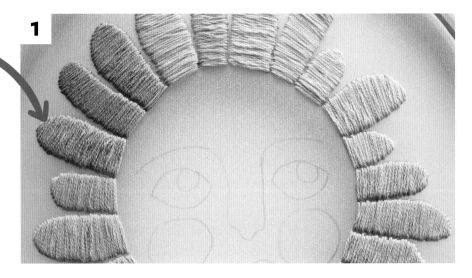

2. The line work of this step requires more precision and care. Using split stitch in shade 924, stitch one row for the nose and outline of the eyes, and stitch two or three rows for the eyebrows; the change in line weight adds to the face's expression. Fill in the pupils with satin stitch.

Note: As you make your lines, work slowly and be sure to carefully hide the tail when you start stitching. When you are ready to snip your thread, simply weave through a few times at the back of the lines you embroidered. If you have any flyaways when you are done, use a very small amount of a product like Dritz® Fray Check® or a fabric glue to smooth them down.

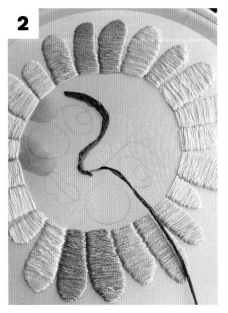

3

3. For the cheeks, use split stitch in 3779 to essentially work in a swirl, starting at the outer edge of each circle and working around until you end in the middle. This process creates movement for the viewer and an intriguing interplay between different textures.

4

4. Stitch the lips with satin stitch in 760 to create two separate shapes for the top lip and bottom lip. This creates a natural shadow where the shapes meet, making the mouth look more realistic.

— BLUE FLOWER LADY PATTERN —

Celestial Garden

Capture the magic of a whimsical sun and moon along with two delicate flower stems. This is the largest design in the book, and the hoop size gives us a lot of room to embroider. I like the mix of bold and detailed shapes in this piece. And this project shows that, even with just a few different stitches, you can create something extravagant!

SUPPLIES
- Thread colors (DMC): 924, ECRU, 3687, 777, 3326, 350, 927, 928, 3852, 725, 3822, 919, 921, 922, 738, 948, 163, 164
- Hoop: 9" (22.9cm)
- Fabric: 11" (27.9cm) square

STITCHES USED
- Satin stitch (see page 28)
- Short and long stitch (see page 30)
- Split stitch (see page 32)

1. Stitch the facial features first. Use split stitch in 924 for the brows on both faces and the nose on the sun, stitching two or three rows for the brows and one row for the nose. Create the whites of the eyes (ECRU), the pupils (924), and the lips (3687 for the moon; 777 for the sun) with satin stitch. For the lips, make two separate shapes (top lip and bottom lip) to create a shadow where they meet and give the mouth a more realistic look. Finally, use split stitch for the cheeks (3326 for the moon; 350 for the sun) Start on the outside of the circle and work inward to create a swirled effect.

Note: Creating the facial features first makes the thread-painting process much easier because you won't have to leave narrow spaces to fill in later—if you start with these details, you can maneuver around them.

2. Use short and long stitch to fill in the moon, starting with 927 on the outer edge. Then use 928 to blend the face toward the nose. Give the edge of the moon a clean look with a split stitch outline in 927.

2

3. For the sun, use short and long stitch in 3852 on the outside of both sides of the face. Next, blend 725 into the stitches you made with 3852, stopping near the middle of the eye on each side. In the center of the face, use short and long stitch in 3822 to fill in the remaining area.

Create the sun's rays with vertical satin stitches in shades 919, 921, 922, and 3852. Complete one color at a time so that you do not have to stop and start with a new color for each ray. To make sure your thread isn't visible as you move between the rays, just flip your hoop over and weave through the back of the face stitches to get to the starting point of the next ray. Finish this step with a split-stitch outline in 919 around the outside of the face.

3

4

4. Finish the design with the two delicate flowers. Begin with the petals, using satin stitch in shade 738 for the top flower and 948 for the bottom flower. Next, create two rows of split stitch for each stem in shade 163. Finally, use satin stitch in 164 to create the leaves.

— CELESTIAL GARDEN PATTERN, COPY AT 200% —

Flower Lady Flowerpot

Stitch a flower arrangement that will never wilt! A fun flowerpot and a fluffy pom-pom make this design bright and whimsical with vivid colors and intriguing textures. A sleeping flower lady watches over this embroidered bouquet and adds a unique element to this stylized still life.

SUPPLIES
- Thread colors (DMC): 798, 996, 758, ECRU, 799, 3765, 3782, 718, 3607, 3733, 3716, 3849, 3817, 954, 725
- Hoop: 8" (20.3cm)
- Fabric: 10" (25.4cm) square

STITCHES USED
- Chain stitch (see page 18)
- Pom-pom (see page 26)
- Satin stitch (see page 28)
- Short and long stitch (see page 30)
- Split stitch (see page 32)

1. Start by stitching the details on the flowerpot. Create the outline of the flower lady's facial features (brows, nose, and eyes) in 798, making two rows of very small split stitches side by side. Use satin stitch for the cheeks (996), lips (798), face (ECRU), and petals around the face (798), then create a split-stitch outline in ECRU around the outside of the face. Make the small flowers on the flowerpot with satin stitch in the following shades: 799 for the top left and bottom right, 996 for the top right and bottom left, and 3765 for the bottom center. Use ECRU for the flower centers.

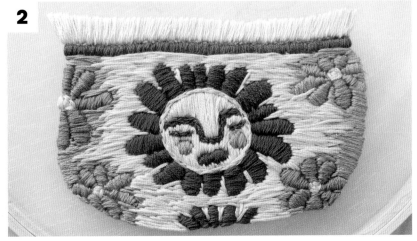

2. Stitch the background of the flowerpot with short and long stitch. Use 3782 on the outer edges and then blend in ECRU to fill in the rest of the pot to create shading and give the pot a rounded effect. To finish this part of the design, make two stripes of satin stitch at the top of the flowerpot: a thin row of vertical stitches in 3765 topped with a thick row of vertical stitches in ECRU.

3

3. It's time to work on the flowers. Start with the petals, rather than the stems, so that you can hide your thread more easily as you start and stop. Stitch the petals in alternating shades of pink: 718 and 3607 for the center flower, and 3733 and 3716 for the outer two flowers.

4

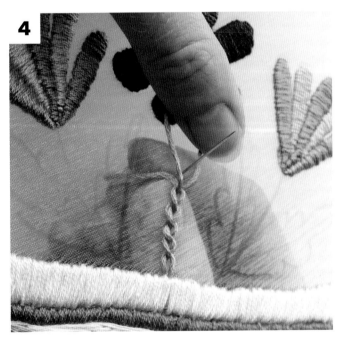

4. To add texture and variety to the piece, stitch the stems with chain stitch. Stitch only the center stem at this point, using shade 3849.

5

6

7

5. Instead of stitching the other stems, stitch the leaves on the outer two flowers, using satin stitch in 3817; this way, you will not stitch over parts of the stem when you make the leaves. For each leaf, create two mirrored sections along the center line by making diagonal stitches, carefully following the scalloped edge of the leaf.

6. Use chain stitch in 954 to make the other two stems. Don't worry about overlapping the points where the two leaves touch at the stem—you are meant to stitch over this part to achieve the desired effect.

7. To create the pom-pom at the center of the middle flower, take a long piece of floss in 725 and wrap it around two fingers about 25 to 30 times. Leave a small tail at the end and wrap it around the center of your looped thread a couple of times, and you are left with something that looks like a bow.

8. Place the looped thread on your fabric where you want to position the pom-pom. Take another long strand of 725, thread your needle, and come up to the front of the hoop by pushing your needle through the middle of your future pom-pom. (Optional: You can use a knot at the end of this floss to secure it at the back, as it will be well covered by the flower and pom-pom.) Make a series of loops at the center of the pom-pom to fill in any gaps and give it a more even, round shape. When you are satisfied with the number of loops, end at the back and snip your excess thread.

9. Cut all the loops and use the tip of your needle to separate the strands of thread. Slowly trim and shape until you have a small, round pom-pom.

Floral Wreath

Delicate with bold structural details, this design is sure to impress! Create a floral wreath that will keep its bright, cheerful colors year-round. The standout feature of this hoop is the raised yellow flower that is created using the woven picot stitch. This stitch is so fun to make, and the result is so rewarding, especially when you finish the petals and see them standing up from the fabric as if they are growing right out of your artwork!

SUPPLIES
- Thread colors (DMC): 321, 554, 602, 164, 581, 904, 420, 924, 777, 3013, 3820
- Hoop: 8" (20.3cm)
- Fabric: 10" (25.4cm) square

STITCHES USED
- Back stitch (see page 16)
- Chain stitch (see page 18)
- French knots (see page 20)
- Satin stitch (see page 28)
- Split stitch (see page 32)
- Woven picot stitch (see steps 7–8 on pages 91–92)

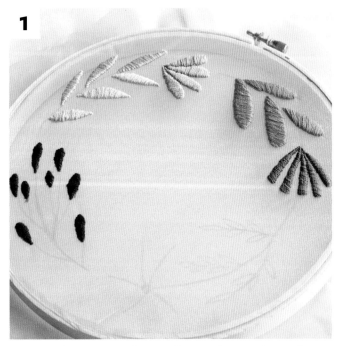

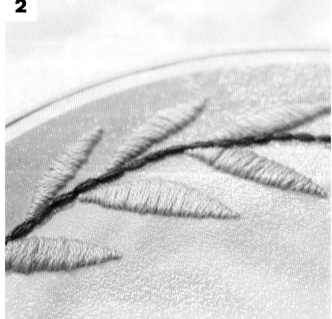

1. Stitch the satin stitch areas first so that you have a large area to work with when finishing the stems and weaving your needle and thread through to end off at the back. Use the following shades: red berries, 321; purple petals, 554; pink petals, 602; leaves of purple flower, 164; and leaves of pink flower, 581.

2. For the stem of the purple flower, stitch a single line in back stitch, starting from the bottom and using shade 904. Leave a tail of thread that you will stitch down as you work on this delicate line. Use your finger to secure the tail as you stitch into the thread. When you reach the petals, weave your needle and thread through a few times and snip the excess.

3

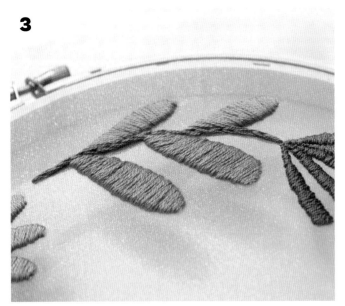

3. Using the same approach as in step 2, create the stem of the pink flower in split stitch with shade 420.

4

4. Use chain stitch in 924 for the berry sprig's stem. As you stitch each line individually, you will have to stop and start each time. To do this, stitch down a small tail of thread and end at each berry by weaving through at the back before cutting off your thread. Work slowly and carefully.

5

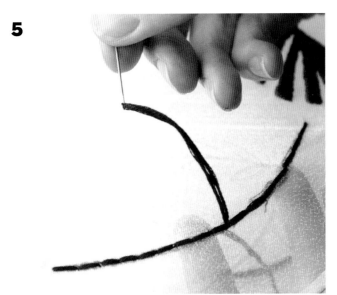

5. For the yellow flower, start with the stem so you don't cover any of the leaves' detail. Using back stitch in 777, stitch the central stem up to the point where each side stem branches off, stitch each segment, and then weave your needle and thread through the back of your stitches to get back to the central stem—this allows you to stitch the stem in one go rather than stitching each branch individually. When you get to the point where the yellow petals will start, weave at the back of the stem because the flower is a raised design element.

6

6. Make the little green leaves with vertical straight stitches in shade 3013. Start in the middle and work your way outward to each side. To stitch all of the leaves without stopping, work side to side on the leaves that mirror each other, then weave through at the back of the stem to get to the leaves at the end of each branch.

7. Create the yellow (3820) flower petals using woven picot stitch. To make this stitch, start by placing a pin in the fabric right where you want the tip of the petal to start. This placement determines the length of each petal. Bring the tip of the needle through so it marks the central line of the petal. Next, thread your needle with a long piece of floss and make a knot at the end. (You can use knots because they will be covered as you work on the flower.) Pull the needle through a short distance away from the pin where you want the base of the petal to be, place your thread behind the top of the pin, and put your needle back through the fabric on the other side, at an equal distance from the pin. Come up again just to the left of the pin, at the base of the petal.

7

8. Wrap the floss behind the pin again (from left to right) and start to weave. Moving from right to left, go under-over-under and then pull the thread taut up toward the top of the petal. From here, be sure to alternate your weaving pattern with each pass. Keep stopping to push the thread up so you won't have any gaps. When you are finished, stitch over the outer thread at the base of the flower to lock it in place. You can end with another knot at the back. (I split the 6-ply strand and tied a double knot.) When you have made all of the petals in this way, remove the pin. Anchor the top petal (closest to the blue stem) with a straight stitch and let the other petals stand off the hoop to create shadows.

9. Fill the center of the flower with French knots using 777.

Thread Color Conversion Chart

Color representations are approximate.

ANCHOR	DMC	COLOR NAME
2	BLANC	White
387	ECRU	Ecru
N/A	25	Ultra Light Lavender
873	154	Very Dark Grape
1030	155	Medium Dark Blue Violet
877	163	Medium Celadon Green
240	164	Light Forest Green
342	211	Light Lavender
1026	225	Ultra Very Light Shell Pink
352	300	Very Dark Mahogany
403	310	Black
19/47	321	Red
110/119	333	Very Dark Blue Violet
118	340	Medium Blue Violet
11	350	Medium Coral
214	368	Light Pistachio Green
374	420	Dark Hazelnut Brown
290	444	Dark Lemon
253/254	472	Ultra Light Avocado Green
96/97	554	Light Violet
281/517	580	Dark Moss Green
280	581	Moss Green
57/63	602	Medium Cranberry
55/62	603	Cranberry
831/956	613	Very Light Drab Brown
88	718	Plum
305	725	Medium Light Topaz
279	734	Light Olive Green
361/366/367/942	738	Very Light Tan
303	742	Light Tangerine
868/882/9575	758	Very Light Terra Cotta
1022	760	Salmon
65	777	Very Dark Raspberry
131/137/142/146	798	Dark Delft Blue
136/145	799	Medium Delft Blue
161	813	Light Blue
22/43/44	815	Medium Garnet

ANCHOR	DMC	COLOR NAME
13	817	Very Dark Coral Red
160	827	Very Light Blue
277	831	Medium Golden Olive
1044	895	Very Dark Hunter Green
258	904	Very Dark Parrot Green
340	919	Red Copper
1003	921	Copper
1003	922	Light Copper
816	924	Very Dark Gray Green
837/848	927	Light Gray Green
274	928	Very Light Gray Green
1011	948	Very Light Peach
203	954	Nile Green
316	970	Light Pumpkin
297	973	Bright Canary
433	996	Medium Electric Blue
842	3013	Light Khaki Green
905	3031	Very Dark Mocha Brown
266	3347	Medium Yellow Green
263	3362	Dark Pine Green
87	3607	Light Plum
25	3716	Very Light Dusty Rose
75	3733	Dusty Rose
1031/1096	3753	Ultra Very Light Antique Blue
170	3765	Very Dark Peacock Blue
167	3766	Light Peacock Blue
1012	3779	Ultra Very Light Terra Cotta
899	3782	Light Mocha Brown
875	3817	Light Celadon Green
306	3820	Dark Straw
305	3821	Straw
295	3822	Light Straw
306	3852	Very Dark Straw
1003	3853	Dark Autumn Gold
1010	3856	Ultra Very Light Mahogany
358	3862	Dark Mocha Beige
376	3864	Light Mocha Beige

About the Author

Sarah Godfrey is an embroidery artist, illustrator, and designer with a passion for color, texture, and the beauty of nature. She is the owner of The Lake of Spring online shop, where she offers downloadable embroidery patterns, art prints, finished hoops, and one-of-a-kind upcycled garments. In 2020, she was selected as the Artist in Residence at the Schneider Haus National Historic Site (Kitchener, Ontario), where her solo exhibition focused on her hand embroidery, block printing, and illustration work. To see more of Sarah's art, visit her on her website (*www.TheLakeofSpring.com*), Etsy (*thelakeofspring*), or Instagram (*@thelakeofspring*). She lives in Ontario, Canada, with her husband and son.

To my husband, Nick, and my son, Ellis. Thank you for your endless love and support. You inspire me every day!